# THE FINAL NESTING PLACE

Creating a Meaningful and
Personal Space for Your Loved
One to Live Their End of Life

## CARRIE CHAVEZ HANSEN

BART PRESS
COLORADO SPRINGS, CO

The Final Nesting Place: Creating a Meaningful and Personal Space for Your Loved One to Live Their End of Life

Copyright © 2012 Carrie Chavez Hansen

Publisher:
Bart Press LLC
Colorado Springs, Colorado

All rights reserved. No part of this publication may be reproduced, stored in a retrieval system, or transmitted in any form or by any means, electronic, mechanical, photocopy, recording, or otherwise without the written permission of the copyright holder or publisher. The scanning, uploading, and distribution of this book via the internet or via any other means without the permission of the publisher is illegal and punishable by law. Purchase only authorized electronic editions, and do not participate in or encourage electronic piracy of copyrighted materials.

ISBN-13: 978-0-9852509-0-4
ISBN-10: 0985250909

ISBN-13: 978-0-9852509-1-1 (e-book)
ISBN-10: 0985250917 (e-book)

Printed in the United States of America

## IN MEMORY OF

Juan Bautista Chavez (1927-1999)
Ophelia M. Chavez (1926-2000)
Baltazar "Blackie" Blackwood (1934-2003)
Danny Lars Hansen (1977-2008)

## DEDICATION

This book is lovingly dedicated to
Janae, Mercedes, Tristan, Antonio and Curtis
Thank you for being the light and laughter
that fills my heart. You are the future of our family
and I am so proud of each one of you.
It is an honor to be part of your lives.
You are the sweetest part of my life story.
*Te amo con todo mi corazon.*

# CONTENTS

INTRODUCTION: My Story     ix

## PART ONE: STORY OF PEOPLE     1

| | | |
|---|---|---|
| one: | **CIRCLE OF LIFE** | 3 |
| two: | **LIFE STORY** | 7 |
| | heritage | 9 |
| | education and occupation | 13 |
| | relationships | 17 |
| | lifestyle | 22 |
| | defining moments | 29 |
| | sensory story | 31 |

## PART TWO: STORY OF PLACE     35

| | | |
|---|---|---|
| three: | **STORYTELLING BY DESIGN** | 37 |
| | style | 38 |
| | color | 41 |
| | furnishings | 43 |
| | texture | 45 |
| | pattern | 48 |
| | lighting | 49 |
| | accessories | 51 |
| four: | **ENGAGING THE SENSES** | 53 |
| | smell | 55 |
| | touch | 57 |
| | sound | 58 |

| | | |
|---|---|---|
| **five:** | **HOME** | 61 |
| **six:** | **HOSPICE FACILITIES** | 67 |
| **seven:** | **NURSING HOMES AND HOSPITALS** | 69 |
| | nursing homes | 70 |
| | community homes | 73 |
| | hospitals | 75 |

## PART THREE: STORY OF THINGS 79

| | | |
|---|---|---|
| **eight:** | **OTHER METHODS OF STORYTELLING** | 81 |
| | personal objects | 82 |
| | photographs | 85 |
| | personal journals | 87 |
| **nine:** | **HEALING ART** | 89 |
| | painting | 90 |
| | music | 91 |
| | movement | 92 |

## PART FOUR: STORY OF MORTALITY 93

| | | |
|---|---|---|
| **ten:** | **DYING IS PART OF LIVING** | 95 |
| | signs of dying | 96 |
| | dying well | 100 |
| | completion of life | 102 |

## PART FIVE: STORY OF YOU 105

**eleven: YOUR STORY** 107
    care of you 108
    growing through grief 109
    honouring your relationship 111

CONCLUSION 113

ACKNOWLEDGMENTS 115

RESOURCES 119

ABOUT THE AUTHOR 121

# INTRODUCTION

*"Life, with the soul predominant is a noble mosaic, a bewitching arabesque."*

EDWIN LEIBFREED

## My Story

Creating meaningful, personal spaces to live, play and work in has been a passion of mine for as long as I can remember. As a young girl, I spent countless hours redecorating and remodelling my tiny metal dollhouse with scraps of carpeting and fabric.

As I grew and evolved from a pig-tailed little girl to a young woman, I began a business career that ultimately placed me in the middle of corporate America. I had set aside my true desire to work in the design field.

After a period of limited personal growth in my life, I realized my truth: The passion for creating beautiful and inspiring spaces courses through my veins, giving me life and energy. It is at the core of my very being. Simply put, *Design is My Truth*.

At the age of thirty, I went back to college. This time I followed my passion and honoured my truth by studying interior design. Since that time and during the years I have worked as a designer, I have continued to learn and evolve both as an artist and as a human being.

On my life journey I have been very fortunate to have the support of a loving family and loyal friends. They have always been there to believe in me and to push me onward whenever life handed me difficult situations.

One set of situations I was not prepared to be handed was that of my mother and brother-in-law each being diagnosed with a form of terminal cancer. I am thankful that they were diagnosed several years apart. However, it did not make accepting their illnesses any easier. Once I was able to reasonably accept what life had presented our family with, I could take action. Because I felt so helpless during their illnesses and at the end of their lives, I had to rely on what had become instinctual to me. Together with other family members I created nurturing and peaceful spaces for them to live their end of life. Doing this not only helped my mother and brother-in-law, but it also helped me. It gave me a purpose, a little bit of control over the situation, and the ability to gift each of them with something extremely personal.

Despite the sheer helplessness we may feel when someone we care about is at the end of life, creating a personal space for them is something tangible and meaningful we can do. But just what does that look like and what does it mean?

For each of my loved ones, this looked very different. For my brother-in-law, this meant creating a refuge in his home in which he could relax and recover from treatments: a comfortable place to rest, a nurturing space to heal, a safe haven to nestle in, and an inviting home to live the rest of his life.

In my mother's situation, the focus was on creating an environment in which she could peacefully spend her last days. This meant providing for her physical needs as well as maintaining a meaningful and personal space for her while allowing nature to gently take its course.

Although each situation was different, the goal was the same: to provide a physically comfortable and appropriate space that felt safe and secure based on what would be personally meaningful to each of them. Providing for physical needs while creating a positive emotional experience is, at its very core, the purpose of interior design.

Whether we are aware of it or not, our environment plays a huge role in how we feel on a daily basis. In most commercial spaces, designers select colors, materials, finishes, and lighting based on how they want us to feel, respond, and act while we are in those spaces. Savvy business owners intentionally create positive responses to help ensure the success of their business. Think about how you feel or respond the next time you visit a restaurant, coffee shop, book store, dentist or physician's office, clothing store, or school.

Interior design in our homes or personal space isn't much different. However, it is based upon meeting our individual needs rather than on the needs and desired response of the general public.

Every person and every situation is unique. We each have our own distinct set of personal circumstances and experiences that make up our life story. It is our individual responses to these experiences and circumstances that have shaped and created the whole of who we are and how we will be remembered.

If your loved one is approaching the end of life, you have the unique opportunity to make a difference in how that precious time is lived. As difficult and daunting as that task may seem, it is absolutely possible. I know this because I have been where you are. It would be wrong to assume that I know how you feel; I don't. But I do understand. This book is written with understanding, compassion and respect for you and your loved one. It is my sincere desire to help you translate your loved one's unique story into a personal and meaningful space—their *final nesting place*.

THE FINAL NESTING PLACE

## part one

# STORY OF PEOPLE

"Live your life from your heart. Share from your heart. And your story will touch and heal people's souls."

MELODIE BEATTIE

CARRIE CHAVEZ HANSEN

## chapter one

## CIRCLE OF LIFE

"*One returns to the place one came from.*"

JEAN DE LA FONTAINE

WHEN WE ARE ABOUT to be born, parents busily prepare for our arrival by creating a space dedicated to our comfort and safety. As a first-time parent, I did everything I could to prepare the perfect space for the new addition to our family. I thought about paint colors, furniture, bedding, lighting, music and much more. I wondered how I would incorporate all of the details into a space that would also keep my baby safe and sound. I searched for the perfect chair in which to sit, feed and soothe my child. I spent hours designing and sewing her crib bedding. All of this preparation and more was done even before she drew her first breath.

I also attended birthing classes so that I could be informed of the physical aspects of giving birth, as well as learn what steps I could take to ensure as pleasant an experience as possible. I was even given instructions on how to breathe during the painful contractions. Another vital step in preparing for the actual birth experience included becoming familiar with the hospital facilities such as the emergency entrance area, nurses' station, maternity ward, birthing rooms, and nursery.

The reason for all the preparation was to create a meaningful and personal experience while in a nurturing and loving environment. When a child enters your life, you make preparations to accommodate them. You want them to *feel* comfortable, nurtured, safe, and secure while at the same time making sure their physical needs are being met. These preparations are commonly referred to as *nesting* and often provide the physical and emotional foundation for the beginning of life.

Knowing that we possess the natural tendency to nest at the beginning of life, it makes sense that we also possess the same tendency or instinct to nest at the end of life. The moments of birth and of death are, universally, two of the most profound and intimate experiences human beings can share with one another. They are both equally significant, yet much more planning goes into creating meaningful environments for those being born than for those who are near death or dying. Each of these moments in our lives is sacred and should be treated as such.

In Western culture, the subject of dying and death is widely considered to be taboo. However, a culture shift has begun in which the silence is being broken, lines of communication are being opened, and language is being spoken in a way that honors those that we love. You can be part of this important culture change. Mindfully preparing a meaningful environment for your loved one at the end of life is a significant step in the right direction.

CARRIE CHAVEZ HANSEN

**chapter two**

## LIFE STORY

"Their story, yours and mine – it's what we all carry with us on this trip we take, and we owe it to each other to respect our stories and learn from them."

WILLIAM CARLOS WILLIAMS

EACH TIME I BEGIN a new interior design project, the first task I embrace is to learn about my clients: their lifestyle, family, personal preferences, needs, etc. This initial phase of the design process is called *programming* and often is accomplished by thoughtfully conducting a detailed personal interview or gathering specific information via a written questionnaire.

I believe programming is more like *story telling*. It captures the *story* of the person you are attempting to help. In order for you to create a personal and meaningful space for your loved one, you first need to consider various aspects of their life story.

For example, where did they grow up? What experiences from their early life relate to who they are now? Do they have a particularly rich cultural background that influences the way they live on a daily basis? Are there particular objects, fabrics, colors that signify their culture? Are there any specific spiritual or religious beliefs that play an important role in their life? Are there any customs or rituals that have been significant or meaningful to them? What about life experiences and work? Did they serve in the military? Is love of country something they value? Do they now or did they have a beloved pet? Are they parents? How do they relate to other people? Who are the important people in their life? What about significant events in their life? Do they have a favorite vacation memory? Or perhaps they have a meaningful life experience that made a deep impact on their life. Do they like to listen to a certain genre of music? Do they have a favorite sound such as waves washing upon a sea shore? What about their state of their health? Where are they on their journey? How old are they? Are they a child, a young adult, middle-aged or older?

When woven together, each of these life details and experiences forms the inimitable story of your loved one. It is important to recognize their story so that you can translate it into meaningful and personal components of their environment. The following sections and subsequent chapters will help you explore the various facets of their story; which will, in turn, provide you with the basis for the creation of their personal sanctuary, their nest.

## heritage

*"In all of us there is a hunger, marrow-deep, to know our heritage, to know who we are and where we came from."*

ALEX HALEY

YOUR LOVED ONE'S HERITAGE is the cornerstone of their life story. It naturally encompasses the most basic elements that influence who they are. What may seem ordinary or inconsequential is actually the very thing that makes your loved one's story so unique, so profound. Yes, we sometimes grow beyond or in spite of our heritage, but it is still a key factor in realizing who we are and where we came from. Embrace your loved one's heritage; it will help you authentically understand them.

*Steve's Story*

Steve has a rich Mexican heritage that includes many diverse cultural elements. One rudimentary, yet significant, element is food. He grew up in a home where the signature spicy aroma of Mexican food being prepared in the kitchen by his mother was a staple in his life. As an adult, he began carrying on the cultural tradition of preparing and serving many of the same foods.

A newly single father, he moved into an apartment and settled in with his three boys. One evening they were all sitting together when the boys told him they were hungry. He didn't have much to eat in the house at the time—some tortillas, beans, cheese and other staples. He made them some simple burritos for dinner. When he had finished cooking, Steve looked at his three boys sitting together sharing a meal and realized, in that poignant moment, *he was home.*

**When thinking of your loved one's unique heritage, consider the following:**

✎ When and where were they born?

✎ Where did they grow up?

- ✎ What was the general atmosphere in the home where they grew up?

- ✎ Did the location of where they were raised influence them? How?

- ✎ Can you think of any other geographical factors that have influenced your loved one?

- ✎ What is their ethnicity and what role does that play in their life?

- What is their cultural background? Are there any specific practices of their culture that are particularly meaningful?


- Are there any personal items or photographs that would represent this time in their life?

## education and occupation

"Be glad of life because it gives you the chance to love and to wcrk and to play and to look at the stars."

HENRY VAN DYKE

AS I SHARED IN the introduction, your education and occupation can have a deep and meaningful impact on your life. Both have positively influenced my life in a number of ways. In the past, I have utilized my business background along with the artistic influences in my design projects. Now, I am combining that with some difficult personal experiences in my life in order to write this book.

Your loved one may have an educational or occupational background that has influenced them in a significant way. Perhaps they have experience as a teacher, coach, truck driver, welder, dog groomer, computer programmer, medical technician, musician, artist, florist, or homemaker. Perhaps they have a proud military background or they may have dedicated a part of their life to volunteering for a favorite cause.

Each choice or decision your loved one made regarding this time in their life makes their story both interesting and unlike any other.

**Some questions to consider for this part of their story:**

- ✍ How has their education influenced them?

- ✍ Are there any volunteer experiences that have influenced them?

- ✍ What vocational experiences have influenced your loved one?

- ✍ Do they have a military background?

- ✍ What branch of the military did they serve in?

- ✍ How did their military experience influence your loved one?

- ✍ Do they have volunteer experience they are particularly passionate about?

- ✍ How has this volunteer experience influenced your loved one?

- ✍ Is your loved one a homemaker?

- Are there aspects of their experience that were meaningful to them? If so, what were they?


- Can you think of any other vocational experiences that may have influenced your loved one?

## relationships

*"Families are united more by mutual stories—of love and pain and adventure—than by biology."*

DANIEL TAYLOR

ESTABLISHING AND NURTURING PERSONAL relationships are at the very core of our being. The power of personal interaction and relationships can have a profound effect on our lives. Of course, there are positive as well as negative experiences associated with any personal relationship. Knowing which relationships have had the most meaning to your loved one is crucial in understanding them.

Relationships are as diverse as those who are a part of them. The primary sets of relationships we have are those with family, friends, and pets.

### FAMILY

In the age of the modern family, the meaning of the word *family* takes on a very personal and individual meaning. For some, family is the people we choose. Let's take a look at those relationships that have had the greatest impact on your loved one.

**When thinking of their close family relationships, consider:**

- What influence have their parents or other family members had upon your loved one?

- Who has been their most important or influential family member?

- What does *family* mean to your loved one?

- Is family important to them?

## FRIENDS

Friendships change and evolve over the course of time like the ebb and flow of water at the ocean's shore. Sometimes we are fortunate enough to have the type of long-lasting friendships that endure a lifetime. Friends share our joys and triumphs, encourage and inspire us to embrace opportunities, protect our deepest secrets, and enrich our lives immeasurably.

**Consider the following questions when thinking of your loved one's friendships:**

- ✍ What have your loved one's personal friendships been like over the years?

- ✍ Who have been the most significant friends in your loved one's life?

- ✍ What friend or friends are currently closest to your loved one?

- ✍ Are there certain friendships that need to be honoured during your loved one's end of life?

- ✍ Does your loved one need to resolve any conflicts or disagreements with an important friend?

## PETS

If your loved one is an animal lover, they may have a beloved personal pet. Their pet may be a cat, dog, bird, or reptile. Perhaps they are a horse lover or fish aficionado. Whatever the case may be, it is important to honor their relationship with animals. Your loved one may consider their pet part of their family.

**Some questions to consider when you are thinking of your loved one's relationships with animals:**

- Are they responsive to animals?

- Do they own a pet? If so, what kind?

- Would it be meaningful or helpful for your loved one to have their pet nearby?

# lifestyle

"Every one of us is a wonder. Every one of us has a story."

KRISTIN HUNTER

## AGE

The age of your loved one at end of life is as individual as they are. Sadly, we are not all fortunate enough to live long, full lives. All too often, precious lives are cut drastically short by unexpected illnesses or circumstances beyond our control. My brother-in-law Danny lived only 30 years. Many live shorter lives than even he. This does not make their lives less important. It does give us, you and me, the responsibility of creating a meaningful space that is uniquely *appropriate* for their individual age and lifestyle. Think of it is a wonderful gift you are giving them.

## HEALTH STATUS

It is very important to consider where your loved one is on their life journey. Knowing their most recent and current health condition can help you determine what their greatest physical needs are and what is most appropriate for their individual circumstances.

- ✐ What is your loved one's current health status?

- ✐ Has their healthcare provider given them an approximate prognosis?

- ✐ What physical expectations does their healthcare provider have for them in the coming months? Weeks? Days?

- ✐ Does your loved one require the use of any special medical equipment?

- ✐ Do they have any known physical limitations you need to be aware of?

✍ Are they on any medication right now? Will you need to administer their medication?

✍ Have they been prescribed pain relief? If not, will they need to receive a prescription for pain relief medication?

✍ Are they able to swallow and take any needed medications?

✍ Is there an alternative plan in place to administer any necessary medication should they be unable to take it orally?

✍ Is Hospice part of their end-of-life care?

## RELIGIOUS AND SPIRITUAL BELIEFS

Whether or not you share your loved one's spiritual or religious beliefs, it is essential to recognize your differences. Treat their beliefs with the utmost respect and a refined sensitivity to what is of value to *them*. There may be specific rituals associated with their belief system that are necessary to honor. They need to feel they are completing their life story in a way that is consistent with their religious or spiritual beliefs.

- ✐ Does your loved one subscribe to any particular religion or belief system? If so, what is it?

- ✐ Were they raised with a certain religious or spiritual belief? If so, how has that influenced their life?

- ✐ Are there any particular rituals that need to be followed in accordance with their beliefs or religion? If so, what are those rituals?

- ✑ Is there a spiritual or religious leader that your loved one would like you to contact on their behalf?

- ✑ Does your loved one believe in prayer?

- ✑ Are there any spiritual end-of-life wishes your loved one needs to express?

- ✑ Does your loved one have any unresolved spiritual or religious issues they may need help with?

# THE FINAL NESTING PLACE

## Ophelia's Story

As Hispanic Catholics, my family had a number of both cultural and religious beliefs surrounding death and dying. My brothers and I took those beliefs into serious consideration when our mother was at the end of her life.

We accounted for everything she would have wanted done for her. We played her beloved Mexican music in the background, lit candles, prayed, gently rubbed dirt on her feet (an ancient cultural custom), and hung rosaries near her bed. On her last day, two close family friends visited, prayed the rosary, and said their good byes to their beloved "Fee." Her religious and cultural beliefs were honored in a way that was personal and meaningful to her. Ophelia's life was complete.

### FAMILY TRADITIONS

Some families have traditions that are passed down from generation to generation. Others have personal traditions they have established within their own family.

- Are there any special family traditions that are meaningful to your loved one? If so, what are they?

✍ Is there a tradition your loved one would like to initiate?

## PERSONAL INTERESTS

✍ Are there any favorite activities your loved one enjoys?

✍ Do they have a favorite pastime that has influenced their life in a positive way?

✍ Are there any personal items that represent their personal interests?

## defining moments

*"The soul needs to tell stories and be listened to."*

THOMAS MOORE

MAJOR LIFE EVENTS OR personally defining moments can have a dramatic influence upon our lives. With this in mind, consider the impact or significance certain events have had on your loved one.

- ✑ What major life events have influenced them?

- ✑ How was your loved one impacted by those events?

- ✑ Do they have a favorite memory that is significant or meaningful to them?

✍ What is a favorite vacation memory they have?

✍ Why is this particular vacation meaningful to them?

## sensory story

*"All we have to believe with is our senses, the tools we use to perceive the world: our sight, our touch, our memory. If they lie to us, then nothing can be trusted. And even if we do not believe, then still we cannot travel in any other way than the road our senses show us; and we must walk that road to the end."*

NEIL GAIMAN

WHEN I WAS A little girl, our family would spend several weekends a year with my Grandma Carrie in the small mountain town of Pagosa Springs, Colorado. I remember, in particular, one bitterly cold winter night. The vintage iron bed I was to sleep in was tucked in a corner right next to a window. The air in the room was fairly cold, especially by the windows as deep snow was pressed against them. When I crawled into bed, my mom and grandma began placing warm quilts and blankets on my small body. As they placed one layer on top of the other, I began to feel the weight of the bedding on my chest and legs. It felt so safe and cozy to have all those blankets and quilts on me; it was as if they were layering their love and warm embraces with each blanket they laid upon me. I felt loved and special.

I never would have imagined that one cold, winter night in my grandma's little house would have such a deep impact on me and my sleeping habits. To this day I love sleeping in a cold room, and nearly every night I will crack open a window to ensure the night's crisp air will fill the space. I also need to have the weight of several layers of bedding on me when I sleep. It doesn't matter what time of year it is; I must sleep with layers on me. The combination of a cool room and heavy bedding feels like *home* to me; it is part of my sensory story.

**What is your loved one's sensory story?**

- Is there a certain sensation that is important or meaningful to them?

- Are there certain textures they respond to in a positive manner?

- Is there a certain way they like to be touched?

- ✎ Do they prefer not to be touched?

- ✎ Is there a certain sensory memory or experience that has influenced them in a meaningful way?

- ✎ What are some of their favorite smells? Are any scents particularly soothing to them?

- ✎ What is their favorite sound?

- ✎ Do they have a favorite genre of music?

CARRIE CHAVEZ HANSEN

THE FINAL NESTING PLACE

## part two

## THE STORY OF PLACE

"Home...is a nest where the soul takes a rest."

FROM <u>THE WIND IN THE WILLOWS</u>

CARRIE CHAVEZ HANSEN

**chapter three**

## STORYTELLING BY DESIGN

"Decorating is not about making stage sets, it's not about making pretty pictures for the magazines; it's really about creating a quality of life, a beauty that nourishes the soul."

ALBERT HADLEY

NOW THAT YOU HAVE identified the key elements of your loved one's story, you can begin transcribing them into a beautiful and unique physical narrative—rich in the meaningful details of their life. This personal narrative is your loved one's *final nesting place*. It is their place of sanctuary: a personal refuge which expresses and reflects their most important and profound life experiences, beliefs, and relationships. When melded together with basic principles of interior design, these individual elements make the space inspiring and meaningful.

Your loved one's *final nesting place* is not meant to be a sterile showcase nor be magazine worthy. It is not about *pretty*; but rather, it is about a creating a meaningful, private haven in which they can rest, reflect, love, and live their end of life.

## style

"I discovered that what's really important for a creator isn't what we vaguely define as inspiration or even what it is we want to say, recall, regret, or rebel against. No, what's important is the way we say it. Art is all about craftsmanship. Others can interpret craftsmanship as style if they wish. Style is what unites memory or recollection, ideology, sentiment, nostalgia, presentiment, to the way we express all that. It's not what we say but how we say it that matters."

FEDERICO FELLINI

YOUR LOVED ONE'S FINAL nesting place should be inviting, casual, comfortable, personal, and special. It should also be relatively versatile and functional. What is important is not a particular decorative style, but rather their individual style based on what is meaningful and personal to them. Start with the foundation of comfortable furnishings; add layers of soft texture, flexible lighting, a variety of pillows, and functional storage. Enhance the space further with meaningful photos, artwork and accessories. Let the style of the space evolve and unfold as you add descriptive layers that express facets of your loved one's *life story*. Allow the space to be a touchstone for the things they love and treasure most, and it will naturally embody their unique personality and style.

# THE FINAL NESTING PLACE

## Danny's Story

Danny was an intelligent, handsome young man who loved life. He was tall and thin, had beautiful blue eyes, wavy brown hair and a brilliant smile. During his 29th year of life, he developed an annoying, persistent cough and noticed that he was often tired and listless. A few months later, he was diagnosed with a germ cell tumor that had grown in his chest. He underwent surgery to remove the tumor and began chemotherapy treatment that lasted a year.

I offered to help his wife paint and decorate their house so that he could have a comfortable space to recover from his treatments. Danny, a devout member of the "beige club," was pretty hesitant about putting color on the walls. It was almost comical the way he was so set in his mind on the color beige. We painted the family room, dining room, and kitchen a warm honey color. The paint immediately set a warm and inviting tone for the house.

Danny and his wife were huge fans of mid-century modern style furnishings and had purchased a beautifully re-upholstered mid-century modern sofa sectional that fit perfectly in the family room. We purchased a round mid-century modern dining table to nestle under a vintage single-globe pendant light fixture we installed. I added layers of books, personal photographs, artwork and more lighting. All of the elements melded together to create the perfect nesting place for Danny. He could lounge on the sofa sectional under layers of soft throws when he was tired and sit at the dining room table for meals or to work on his laptop whenever he needed.

He flashed his signature toothy grin when everything was completed, letting me know he was happy with the finished space. The walls were a deeper shade of "beige" than he expected; but he was pleasantly surprised. Their home went from a reasonably comfortable, colorless space to a stylishly warm, inviting haven from the life storm that had become part of Danny's story.

## color

*"Emotions are the colors of the soul."*

WM. PAUL YOUNG, <u>The Shack</u>

COLOR IN ITSELF IS profound; it instantly establishes the mood and emotional temperature of a space. It can make the difference between a room feeling drab, dark and uninviting to it feeling light, airy, and welcoming. You give a space those characteristics by selecting a color that evokes certain emotional responses. When thinking about color for your loved one's final nesting place, decide what mood you want to create in the space—serene, soothing, spirited, cheerful, or peaceful. Make it soulful and something that speaks directly to their heart.

Colors have soul and depth. Red and orange exude warmth and power and make us feel energized, blue has a soothing effect and suggests trust, green and grey also have calming effects and help us concentrate, pastel colors calm and exude tranquility, yellow makes us feel warm and happy, while purple suggests inspiration and creativity.

There is, of course, a science behind how certain colors make you feel. However, I believe your color choice should be personal as well. The key, then, is focusing on your loved one's individual reaction to color. Perhaps they feel best in cool blue rooms or prefer to spice things up with a warm terra-cotta hue. You can also look to their wardrobe for clues regarding personal color preference.

Keep in mind that both natural and artificial light can have a dynamic effect on color. When selecting paint colors, purchase small sample amounts of your color choices. Paint a large (at least 3' x 3') sample of each color on the wall of the room you are going to be painting, and watch how light affects the color throughout the day and evening.

There are other ways to introduce color into their space as well. Use flexible neutral tones as your base and add pops of color in fabrics, artwork and accessories. By introducing color in this manner, you can test the waters to see if you or your loved one responds positively.

The colors you choose should reflect their individual preferences and contain elements of their life story. Select colors they love and that have personal meaning. Do not worry about rules or pleasing the masses; instead, trust your instinct and do what feels right for your loved one.

## furnishings

*"We shape our dwellings, and afterwards our dwellings shape us."*

WINSTON CHURCHILL

FURNISHINGS ARE THE PRINCIPLE pieces that establish a living space. Furnishings in your loved one's final nesting place ought to be functional, versatile, and comfortable. Whenever possible, they should also provide a sense of personal history and character. This enriches the room and gives it soul.

Begin with an essential piece of furniture—a bed, sofa or daybed. It will help set the tone for the rest of the space. Depending upon your loved one's own circumstances, this may necessitate the use of a hospital bed. Additional furniture items may include a side table, seating, a storage piece, and a small desk and chair.

Consider side tables as opportunities for adding unique character and whimsy to the space. Look at well-loved items that can be repurposed for use as a table such as a trunk, cart, filing cabinet, wooden side chair, bench or stool. You can also stack a collection of vintage suitcases, hat boxes or books to create a side table. Use items that have personal meaning for your loved one.

For practicality, ensure the top surface area has enough space for daily necessities such as drinks, toiletries and any necessary medications. If your loved one is mobile, ensure the side table is sturdy enough should they need to use it for stability.

When selecting seating for the space, consider adding comfortable pieces that are multi-functional. You may want to include a comfortable chaise lounge, sofa, oversized chair and ottoman, or daybed for lounging during the day and sleeping near your loved one at night.

A small dining table or desk provides an eating and work surface or an area to play games or build puzzles. Add a few light-weight chairs for use around the table or desk; they can also be used as additional seating for guests.

If space allows, an armoire or dresser is the perfect storage solution for fresh linens, towels, sumptuous throws, extra pillows, blankets, and clothing. It also provides an additional surface for lighting, books, favorite photographs and keepsakes.

Feel free to mix and match styles and eras when furnishing your loved one's space. You are creating a distinctive combination that echoes their personal story, their inimitable style.

---

*Don't forget about outdoor space. A comfortable chair or bench outside a front door is the perfect place for them to sit and be connected to the outside world.*

## texture

*"The home should be the treasure chest of living."*

LE CORBUSIER

AN INTIMATE, PERSONAL SPACE such as your loved one's final nesting place invites the literal use of texture to further enhance the space and give it depth, warmth, and interest. Texture can be hard or soft, heavy or light, physical and/or visual. It can be introduced in the room through carved wood furnishings or accessories, woven baskets or furniture, textiles and leather, natural or man-made objects, and any combination of the above.

Hard surfaces or lines can be softened by adding soft or natural textures. Think sumptuous pillows, time-softened quilts, cozy woven throws, and warm wool rugs underfoot. Take this opportunity to layer the room with family heirlooms or other items with personal meaning. The space becomes more interesting and rich with elements from your loved one's story when you add texture.

One of my personal spaces is my home office. It is where I sit as I write these pages. Yes, it serves a very specific purpose in that it provides me a dedicated space to work and write. It also provides me with rich inspiration as I am surrounded with elements from my life story that are textural and meaningful. There are primarily hard surfaces in the space, such as my desk, filing cabinet and bookcases. I have softened the space by adding a patterned thick wool rug under my upholstered chair and a woven chenille throw I keep on my lap. Tattered and gently worn books passed down from my father have been lovingly placed atop the file cabinet alongside a vintage dress form that is home to my mother's silk Korean quilted jacket—a gift from my father during his military service in the United States Navy.

The bookshelves house a small collection of books, personal photographs, a pair of loosely woven baskets to corral magazines and office supplies, a trio of tiny bird nests that give a nod to whimsy and nature, some colorful pottery, and beautiful metal scrolled bookends. The walls have been given dimension and texture through the addition of shadow boxes which display hand-carved southwestern jewelry, a woven rattan and bamboo bulletin board I use as my vision board, a large carved wooden medallion, and a metal cutout of a tree of life with three birds nestled among the branches that represent my three children.

On my desk: I keep another nest for earrings and bracelets, an assortment of picture frames for personal photos of my children and pets, a woven file basket with colorfully patterned file folders, and a woven leather box where I keep current projects. My office has history, depth, and soul.

## THE FINAL NESTING PLACE

Your loved one's final nesting place should have history, depth, and soul. Create a space that is comfortable and warm by incorporating soft linens, textured fabrics, bedding, and a variety of texture. Trust your instinct, be creative, and honor their story.

## pattern

*"No pattern should be without some sort of meaning."*

WILLIAM MORRIS

INTRODUCING PATTERN INTO YOUR loved one's space establishes energy. The pattern can be soft and subtle, bold and dynamic, small or large scale, monotone or multicolored. Look to your loved one's heritage, interests, and other facets of their life story for inspiration. You can introduce pattern through fabrics, rugs, flooring, wall coverings or stencils, tapestries, artwork, flags, photographs, and personal collections. It is another opportunity to be creative and add meaningful and personal elements into your loved one's space.

# lighting

*"It's not what you look at that matters, it's what you see."*

—HENRY DAVID THOREAU

LIGHTING ESTABLISHES MOOD. IT can be subtle, intimate, or dramatic. Lighting also provides illumination where you need it most. There are three categories of lighting to consider:

- **Ambient** – general or overall light; overhead fixtures or sunlight;
- **Task** – focused light on a specific activity such as reading, handwork, or writing; table and floor lamps;
- **Accent** – creates drama; often used to illuminate artwork or draw focus on a particular object or wall.

One of the most simple and effective ways to control lighting is by installing dimmer switches. You can also diffuse lighting by installing sheer drapery on windows. The key is to have flexibility when lighting your loved one's room. You will definitely need general or ambient lighting and task lighting in their space. You can also bring in candles or use mirrors to reflect light.

Whenever possible, the room should have windows, preferably on two different walls. Allowing natural light to fill a room brings a sense of warmth and energy and enhances the overall mood of the space. A well-lit space has varying layers, levels, types and sources of light. Consider the specific needs your loved one has for lighting and implement them through the use and placement of different fixtures throughout the space.

## accessories

*"... our objects, bibelots, whatnots, and knickknacks-say the most about who we are. They are as honest as a diary."*

CHARLOTTE MOSS

ACCESSORIES GIVE A ROOM soul. They imbue personality and style. Accessories can also unify a space through color, shape, texture, pattern, or style.

The key is to bring meaning and life into the space; go with what is most meaningful to your loved one—whatever they love. Focus on telling their story through the use of accessories; it can be a profound approach to enriching and enlivening their personal space. What better way to convey the hallmarks of their personal history than through your loved one's personal treasures.

You can also use accessories to introduce whimsy into their space. I believe every room should have a touch of whimsy whether it is an unusual collection, a seashell from a favorite vacation, or a handmade art project from a child. The more unexpected and unique it is, the more character and wit it provides.

Take liberties when displaying accessories. Be creative; set things on the floor, atop a table or dresser, or on walls. Go for the unexpected and hang favorite treasures from the ceiling using invisible fishing line. Unless things are in pairs, select an odd number of things to display together—preferably in threes or fives. It is the most pleasing and natural to the eye.

Do what feels right; once again, don't worry about breaking any design rules. Surround your loved one with things they love and relate to, and you will be successful. Let the accessories be the narrator of their personal story.

## four

## ENGAGING THE SENSES

*"Nothing can cure the soul but the senses, just as nothing can cure the senses but the soul."*

OSCAR WILDE

YOU CAN CREATE A tranquil and enriching environment for your loved one's final journey. The important components of creating such a space are some of the senses themselves: smell, touch, and sound. At perhaps no other time is their sense as heightened and significant to peace and well-being than at the end of life. Remember to take their sensory story into consideration.

## Anna's Story

Anna's idea of the ultimate vacation was a trip to Hawaii. Knowing that her end of life was nearing and that she would not be able to fulfill her travel wish, her hospice team prepared an in-home Hawaiian experience for her. They paid close attention to the sights, scents, sounds, taste and texture that would help foster the feeling of an authentic tropical atmosphere. They began by bringing in large tropical plants and decorations, playing native Hawaiian music, and serving specialty drinks. Whenever friends and family visited Anna, they wore tropical style clothing and leis. One person even built her a custom, heated sand box so that she and others could put their toes in the sand as if on the beach. Even though she was unable to travel to Hawaii, Anna's hospice team was able to bring Hawaii to her in a personal and meaningful way. I can only imagine what an exhilarating, profound experience it was to sit "on the beach" with her toes in the sand, sipping a tropical drink, and sharing the time with those closest to her.

I love this story! It demonstrates perfectly that the experience of creating a personal sanctuary can be fun, inspirational, and unique when it is based upon the individual preferences and story of your loved one.

## smell

*"Smell is a potent wizard that transports you across thousands of miles and all the years you have lived."*

HELEN KELLER

SMELL CAN INSTANTANEOUSLY RECALL a memory or a sense of place. It has the power to soothe and relax our spirit. Pleasing aromas provide a sense of calm and wellbeing. Ancient civilizations often used essential oils and aromatic perfumes in preparation for their loved ones to complete their lives. Today, aromatherapy can help reduce stress for both you and your loved one. Knowing their sensory story will help you implement the use of aromatherapy for your loved one.

**Here are a few simple yet effective ways to incorporate aromatherapy into their end-of-life experience:**

- Gently rub lightly scented lotion onto their skin. This can be any scent they are particularly fond of.
- Place a few drops of essential oils on their bedding but far away enough from their nose so as not to interfere with personal comfort. Lavender essential oil is a fragrance that is especially soothing.

- Light a scented candle nearby.
- Bring in fresh cut flowers and place them in a visible location. Make sure they are not allergic.
- Place lightly scented balm on their lips.
- Avoid wearing perfume or cologne whenever you are around your loved one. This may interfere with the soothing effects other scents can provide.

## touch

*"Sometimes, reaching out and taking someone's hand is the beginning of a journey. At other times, it is allowing another to take yours."*

VERA NAZARIAN

THERE IS NOTHING MORE powerful than the human touch. It connects us to each other on an intimate level. Touch lets us know we *matter*. The importance of touch on a regular basis with your loved one cannot be underestimated. A gentle touch can provide them with feelings of reassurance, peace, solace, and love. Holding their hand in yours and offering encouragement can give them needed strength. Receiving a soothing massage by a qualified massage therapist may provide them with relief from muscle stiffness and pain. Consider other ways to interact with your loved one through physical touch.

## sound

*"Put your ear down close to your soul and listen hard."*

ANNE SEXTON

THE AUDITORY SENSE IS extremely profound. Sound has the power to calm a person's emotional state as well as agitate it. Sound can alert you to danger, dance music, and the dinner bell. Sound is so complex that it staggers the imagination. Music, birds singing, dogs barking, a child crying, dishes clashing in the kitchen sink, a plane flying overhead, fingers drumming on a tabletop, chalk clacking upon a chalkboard, leaves rustling in the wind, bellowing laughter echoing down a hallway, waves washing upon the shore, and friends speaking to one another are only a minute fraction of the sounds you might hear on any given day.

Hearing is widely believed to be the last sense a person retains. That being said, it makes sense for you to honor your loved one's sense of hearing and pay it special attention. Consider the various aspects of their story to help you decide what sounds are appropriate for their environment. If they love the sound of the ocean or a certain genre of music, play it for them. If they are a former teacher or lover of poetry, read favorite passages to them. If they grew up in the city and love the rhythm of that atmosphere, open the windows wide and let the sound permeate their room.

If they are a huge sports fan, share the latest draft picks with them. Remember to keep speaking to them in a tone that is comforting and reassuring. Often, the familiar cadence of a loved one's voice is the most comforting and cherished sound.

Overall, do what is appropriate for them and their unique situation. As end of life approaches, be conscious of creating a soothing environment by keeping sounds low and soft. Be comforted yourself in the knowledge that you are creating a loving and sacred space for your loved one to live their end of life.

## Ophelia's Story

There was a group of local female musicians that my mother loved hearing perform. She told my brother she wanted them to sing at her memorial. He was close friends with one of the musicians and told her about our mother's wish. They agreed to sing but decided not to wait to perform for her. The women (all sisters) came to my mother's house one beautiful afternoon. They strummed their guitars and sang several beautifully harmonious tunes for her. It was such a joyous occasion filled with music, love, and laughter. What an amazing gift it was to see our mother enjoying herself and listening to the music she loved so much. I will be forever grateful to these women for their selfless and beautiful act of kindness.

## chapter five

## HOME

*"The ache for home lives in all of us, the safe place where we can go as we are and not be questioned."*

MAYA ANGELOU

THE ROOM YOU OR your loved one selects for their final nesting place is what is most appropriate for their unique situation. Perhaps that is in their bedroom, a main living area, or a private spot tucked away from the chaos of everyday life. It is also important to ensure their physical needs are met depending upon where they are in their journey.

Armed with details of their life story and some basics of interior design, you can begin creating their personal haven. Be aware of the space requirements you need for furnishings and any medical equipment.

**Think of what works best for your loved one and what makes the most sense:**

- If you are changing the color of the space, you will need to paint first.

- Do some quick measuring to make sure items fit where you would like to place them.
- Arrange larger pieces of furniture keeping in mind the function of each item. Place their bed or major seating facing the entrance and in an area that will provide a view of outside.
- Add or arrange any smaller or secondary pieces of furniture.
- Incorporate any necessary task and ambient lighting.
- Start layering in storytelling elements of color and texture.
- Don't forget to add an element of humor or whimsy.

Remember to be creative, intentional, and flexible as you create a meaningful space that authentically reflects your loved one and their life story.

# THE FINAL NESTING PLACE

## Ophelia's Story

My mother lived in a small three-bedroom 1909 brick bungalow she and my dad had shared since the mid 1970's. Their bedroom was similarly small and located around an awkward corner and away from the rest of the house. Because of this, we decided to move her nesting space into the family dining room. Although this may seem like an odd choice, it made perfect sense to us for a number of reasons. It was:

- the largest room in the house;
- centrally located;
- the room with the most natural light; and
- most importantly, it was a room she was familiar with and one that had very personal meaning.

Over the course of approximately twenty-five years, our family had celebrated countless birthdays and holidays in that room. It is where we gathered to eat our daily meals, play cards and board games, talk over coffee, build puzzles, complete homework, build tablecloth and blanket forts under the table, and so much more.

The lower portion of the walls was covered with light wood paneling and the upper portion with damask wallpaper that my parents had installed themselves. The decorative molding and trim had been painted a bright white by my mother the previous year.

Two windows on each of the outside walls spilled natural sunlight into the room and offered a glimpse into the shade covered yard. A unique vintage copper chandelier that spoke of the home's early history hung over the mid-century dining table.

The space had been decorated sparingly; but you never noticed it, because it had been filled with a quarter century of laughter and joy. The dining room had been the heart of our home and it seemed only natural that it became our mother's *final nesting place.*

**When thinking about the placement of your loved one's nest at home consider:**

✎ What will be the most convenient location?

✎ What is their current health status?

✎ What is the most meaningful area of the home?

- ✎ Do you need to accommodate visitors?

- ✎ Are there windows in the room to provide natural light and a view to the outside?

- ✎ Is the area easily accessible for any necessary healthcare providers?

- ✎ Do you need to accommodate any special medical equipment?

- ✎ Are there any other considerations you need to think about?

CARRIE CHAVEZ HANSEN

## chapter six

## HOSPICE FACILITIES

*"Peace - that was the other name for home."*

KATHLEEN NORRIS

IN-PATIENT HOSPICE FACILITIES are dedicated to the end-of-life care of our loved ones. Hospice honors and values the dying process. They offer comprehensive comfort care to ensure a positive completion of life. All aspects of care are focused on creating a nurturing and meaningful experience. This includes meeting practical, personal, and spiritual needs of both patient and loved ones.

Private and community areas alike are specifically designed with the intent of creating spaces rich in a sense of peace and solace. This has been done by carefully combining elements of color, texture, pattern and lighting. Knowing the profound effect sight, sound, smell, and touch have on our sensory well-being, hospice facility designers have intentionally included features that speak to those needs. These spaces are often nature inspired and may include atriums, aviaries and aquariums.

Incorporating personally significant elements of your loved one's life story into their private hospice room should be welcomed and encouraged. The addition of these elements personalizes the space.

Some facilities have created special areas that honor the military aspect of our loved ones' lives. Hospice realizes the importance and significance their military experience and story have on their personal psyche. Therefore, their story of service, honor, and pride of country is respected and celebrated.

**chapter seven**

## NURSING HOMES AND HOSPITALS

*"After nourishment, shelter and companionship, stories are the thing we need most in the world."*

PHILIP PULLMAN

PLACE IS AS MUCH sensory as it is physical. It is a tangible space and yet it is also a feeling. When creating a *final nesting place* in a nursing home or hospital, you will need to consider the *feelings* you want the room to convey. More than likely, you will want to create a sense of warmth, familiarity, peace, and comfort. In essence, you are creating a sense of *home*.

Of course, you must take the physical aspects of the place into consideration as well. The location of your loved one's nesting place is unique to their individual situation. Create a personal haven for your loved one based on what is relevant and meaningful to them.

## nursing homes

"Home. That wonderful place I was lucky enough to revisit no matter how short a time finally realizing it's not relegated to just one single place its wherever you make it."

ALYSON NOEL,

Blue Moon

IF YOUR LOVED ONE is living their end of life in a nursing home, you have the ability to make a difference in their environment. It has become, after all, their *home*. Do not be afraid to personalize the space with meaningful photos and artwork, favorite quilts or throws. Give the room soul by adding color and texture. Whenever possible, it should express what is familiar and most meaningful to them, their *story*. Check with nursing home staff to see what their guidelines are for personalizing space.

It's important to create an intimate and nurturing environment for your loved one. Take into consideration privacy issues if they share their room with another resident. As your loved one gets closer to completing their life, you may consider asking the staff for more privacy. Perhaps they would be willing to have your loved one's roommate relax in a common area for a few hours.

If possible, enlist the help of hospice in ensuring the comfort and wellbeing of your loved one. They can provide any necessary pain management, additional nursing care, and essential respite for you. Be an advocate for your loved one. Create a sacred and meaningful space for them. It matters.

## Mida's Story

Mida was a naturally beautiful and petite woman born and raised in Texas. She married her college sweetheart and began a family with her young husband. They raised their children to adulthood who in turn began families of their own.

Mida was unexpectedly diagnosed with Alzheimer's disease while in her early fifties. Over the course of fifteen years, Mida's condition progressed leaving behind an ever beautiful and sweet woman with very little, if any, memory of the life she had once known.

Her family made the difficult decision to move her into a nursing home so that she could receive the around-the-clock care she needed.

Mida's daughter Kathy, a seasoned interior designer, understood the intricacies and significance of using her expertise to assist her mom while in the nursing home environment. When Mida was reaching the end of her life, Kathy came to her side to help create a sanctuary for her beloved mother. Since Mida shared her room with another resident, there was a limited amount of privacy available. Kathy instinctively pulled the track curtains around Mida's bed to create a more intimate and private setting. She played soothing music for her mom, turned off the overhead fluorescent lights, and lit a scented candle to create a soft glow. Kathy arranged for a hospice volunteer to give her mom a gentle massage. She also asked the nurses to position Mida on her side so that Kathy could lie next to her.

When Mida drew her last breath, Kathy was lying alongside her precious mother in the heart of the private sanctuary she had created for her.

## community homes

*"I long, as does every human being, to be at home wherever I find myself."*

MAYA ANGELOU

THERE ARE OTHER ALTERNATIVES to nursing homes and assisted living facilities. Holistic Community Living (HCL) is a fairly new community-based residential home living concept dedicated to providing personal holistic care to aging and frail residents. HCL's philosophy provides for their residents to live joyous, meaningful lives within a loving and supportive community. HCL's first residential home is located in Denver, Colorado, and has accommodations for up to twelve residents.

In line with HCL's philosophy and mission, the residential home is located in a thriving neighborhood whose community members support the efforts of the Holistic Community Living's team by volunteering their time. HCL's home offers permanent residence and believes in integrating memory loss residents into their family style setting. It is an intimate and comfortable living environment. Each resident is provided with the opportunity to integrate personal experiences or belongings into their space, their *story*.

I love the concept of this program. It offers an alternative to nursing homes or other assisted living facilities. Holistic Community Living opens its doors to aging or frail individuals and enfolds them into a family style home where residents can choose to live their end of life with joy and dignity.

## hospitals

*"Peace and rest at length have come*
*All the day's long toil is past,*
*And each heart is whispering, 'Home,*
*Home at last."*

THOMAS HOOD

CREATING A FINAL NESTING place in a hospital setting has some intrinsic challenges. In general, there is lack of privacy and intimacy, and the focus is on *medical* care rather than on *personal* care. There is also a certain level of activity and noise that is part of a hospital environment.

The addition of palliative care and/or hospice care can certainly create a more *personal* focus on your loved one. Palliative care is medical care which concentrates on comfort and quality of life for our loved ones. Hospice is personalized end-of-life care that focuses on preparing and helping our loved ones have a positive experience in completing their life. Communicate with your loved one's physician and nurses regarding the availability of hospice care.

It is up to us to create a nurturing and meaningful environment for our loved ones when they are hospitalized. If possible, integrate personal items that are meaningful and that reflect or express their *story*. Incorporating elements from their sensory story can provide them with a sense of familiarity and comfort.

Most importantly, continue speaking to them. Offer comfort, hold their hand, and affirm your feelings for them. Give them the gift of a personal and meaningful experience knowing you are by their side.

# THE FINAL NESTING PLACE

## John's Story

While staying in the hospital overnight for observation, my father died unexpectedly of a heart attack. There was no time for nesting; he was just gone. I spoke with him on the telephone a mere seven hours before he slipped away. He was in really good spirits that evening and was looking forward to breakfast in the morning (he actually loved hospital food). We said good night and that we would speak again tomorrow.

"I love you Dad."

"I love you too Baby Daughter, very much."

Those were the last words we spoke to one another. I was devastated the following morning when I learned of his death. I did take comfort knowing he was in a place that was comfortable and familiar to him. As a chronic back patient, he was often hospitalized for surgeries, traction and other treatments. In the end, it seemed fitting that he spent his last hours in a place he had come to know as kind of a second home. I find solace knowing he felt safe and that our final words were *I love you*.

We don't always have the opportunity to plan ahead and create a final haven for our loved one. When the opportunity does present itself, embrace it. You have been given a gift. It may be a "smack you upside the head" kind of gift; but it is a gift nonetheless.

THE FINAL NESTING PLACE

## part three

## STORY OF THINGS

*"We are shaped and fashioned by what we love."*

GOETHE

CARRIE CHAVEZ HANSEN

**chapter eight**

## OTHER METHODS OF STORYTELLING

*"Increasingly, I realized that I could not merely tell his story. Rather, I would have to tell my story about him."*

RONALD STEEL

HAVING THEIR FAVORITE OR most treasured items surrounding them can have a meaningful impact on your loved one's well-being. Their personal treasures can create a sense of familiarity, security, and belonging. The personal significance of such treasures cannot be overlooked.

What's most important is that which is most meaningful to them. Honor the story within your loved one and help them express or tell that story.

## personal objects

*"The human soul needs actual beauty more than bread."*

D.H. LAWRENCE

I HAVE A FEW prized possessions that I would be hard pressed to ever part with. Each of these items is seemingly common and ordinary. Among my common and ordinary treasures are a typewriter, a pair of cameras, a film projector, sweater, jacket, photographs, and a few pieces of jewelry. I don't know that any one of them even has a significant monetary value; but to me each of them is priceless.

What makes them beautiful and significant to me are the *stories* buried deep within, giving my things soul. Yes, *my typewriter has soul.* It doesn't look very special or soulful from the outside. In fact, it is a beast: a metal Remington Rand manual typewriter that must weigh at least fifty pounds, with the carriage return itself weighing five pounds. It is big, black, old and dusty; and the keys are jammed together, with a few letters missing from the keyboard.

So just where does the soul lie within this broken down old beast? First of all, it belonged to my dad. He was a wordsmith by nature, a printer by trade. Before he died, he wrote a family history book using the ribbon that sits in the heart of the machine. That tattered and worn spool of ribbon holds every stroke, every letter, and every word my dad wrote. The story of my father's family immigrating to Colorado from Spain, and being among the first families to settle in the historic San Luis Valley in 1851 lies inside the old typewriter. It literally holds within it my dad's personal story, his soul. Yes indeed, *my typewriter has soul*.

Things or objects do matter when they tell a story. Contrary to popular belief or rules of design, it is not important that your things are beautiful; what matters most is the soul that lies *within* the item. Good design integrates the things you hold most dear into a space that is personal and altogether beautiful.

✎ What things do you or your loved one have that hold personal meaning?

✎ What special item tells a meaningful story?

- ✐ Does an object remind you of a special time in your life that makes you smile?

- ✐ What things would your loved one consider to have soul?

- ✐ What is the story behind their soulful item?

## photographs

*"It is one thing to photograph people. It is another to make others care about them by revealing the core of their humanness."*

PAUL STRAND

PHOTOGRAPHS HAVE STORIES TO tell; stories of time gone by, momentous occasions, cherished family and friends, beloved pets, places you or your loved one have traveled to or ones dreamt about. Photos capture moments in time that may otherwise be forgotten; they are the most simple and literal way to tell your loved one's story. Display their photographs with freedom and abandon.

### Mida's Story

Mida had endured Alzheimer's disease for about twenty years. Realizing that the nursing home staff had no way of really knowing Mida, her daughter Kathy made a large photo collage of Mida's life—her *story*. Kathy gathered a number of black-and-white photographs of her mother when she was a young woman and placed them lovingly on a board to hang above Mida's bed. The story board provided an inside glimpse of the woman Mida was and helped the nursing home staff learn more about the person they were caring for on a day-to-day basis.

## personal journals

*"We write to taste life twice, in the moment and in retrospect."*

ANAÏS NIN

THE PRACTICE OF JOURNALING captures our present thoughts and feelings providing a source of remembrance and depth of truth. The use of journals tangibly and profoundly narrates our loved one's story.

**Consider having them share:**

- Personal thoughts and feelings about their life
- Notes of forgiveness and love
- Wishes for future of loved ones
- What they are most proud of
- What has been most meaningful to them
- How they want to be remembered

You can also ask visitors, loved ones, and anyone else that wishes to write personal messages in the journal. Your loved one's personal journal provides an opportunity to leave a written legacy of their life.

## CARRIE CHAVEZ HANSEN

## nine

## HEALING ART

*"Creativity healed me. I don't know that I could think of any word that I get more inspired by than the word healing."*

SARK

ART HAS THE POWER to heal. Its source can be storytelling, painting, dancing, music, or visual art; the creative process can have a profound effect on your loved one's mental, emotional and spiritual state. It provides the opportunity to heal spirit, mind and body. Overall, art increases your loved one's sense of well-being and enhances their life.

## painting

*"I dream of painting, and then I paint my dream."*

VINCENT VAN GOGH

### Fred's Story

Fred was a general handyman and house painter who enjoyed crafting alien masks out of fiberglass resin and painting faces on them with fluorescent paint. After being diagnosed with terminal liver disease, he began painting mannequin heads and masks to fill his room, his nest. He painted the walls of his room with fluorescent paint and hung black lights to make all of the paint and figures come to life. He would paint every day, and lie in his room at night staring at his living, ever changing piece of art until he fell asleep. He loved being in the space he had created for himself and lived there through the end of his life.

## music

*"Music gives a soul to the universe, wings to the mind, flight to the imagination and life to everything."*

PLATO

### Henry's Story

Before Alzheimer's disease robbed him of much of his memory, Henry was a charismatic man who enjoyed dancing and listening to music. As his disease progressed, he spent most days idle and unresponsive in a nursing home. Representatives of the Music & Memory iPod Project loaded an iPod with music from Henry's favourite era. They had him listen to the music with earphones, and watched for a response. Henry's eyes opened up wide; he began moving to the rhythm and singing! How profound to see him enjoying himself and engaged! When asked about the music, he responded *"It makes me feel love."* Music was able to connect Henry to his life story and improve his quality of life.

## movement

*"Everything in the universe has a rhythm, everything dances."*

MAYA ANGELOU

AS LONG AS YOUR loved one feels well enough to participate in physical activity, offer them the opportunity to do so. Activities can vary depending upon their limitations and desires. Perhaps a relaxing afternoon of fishing by a small pond, taking a walk, or playing a game of cribbage interests them. They may enjoy yoga, dance, group exercise, or a stroll in the garden. Wherever their interests lie, take the opportunity to honour your loved one's need for movement even if it is simply a short walk to sit outside and enjoy fresh air.

## part four

## STORY OF MORTALITY

"Carve your name on hearts, not tombstones. A legacy is etched into the minds of others and the stories they share about you."

SHANNON L. ALDER

CARRIE CHAVEZ HANSEN

**chapter ten**

## DYING IS PART OF LIVING

*Let children walk with Nature, let them see the beautiful blendings and communions of death and life, their joyous inseparable unity, as taught in woods and meadows, plains and mountains and streams of our blessed star, and they will learn that death is stingless indeed, and as beautiful as life.*

JOHN MUIR

DYING IS AN INTEGRAL part of our life stories. It is an especially important and poignant time in our lives and the lives of our loved ones. Sharing this precious time with your loved one is an opportunity to enrich their end-of-life experience. It is an incomparable honour and privilege for you to be part of their experience.

How your loved one dies matters. They should be reasonably comfortable, know they are not alone, have their wishes honoured, and live the end of their life with respect, dignity, and authenticity.

## signs of dying

"A dying man needs to die, as a sleepy man needs to sleep, and there comes a time when it is wrong, as well as useless, to resist."

STEWART ALSOP

KNOWING THAT DEATH IS soon approaching can be frightening and overwhelming. Learning to recognize some of the most common stages of the end-of-life process can help you cope and know what to expect. Think of the signs and stages as stepping stones along the pathway towards the final destination of your loved one's life journey.

### ONE TO THREE MONTHS BEFORE DEATH

- Withdrawal from world and people
- Decreased food intake
- Increase in sleep
- Going inside of self
- Less communication

## ONE TO TWO WEEKS

- Agitation and restlessness
- Pulling at bedding or clothing
- Disorientation and confusion
- Visions of loved ones
- Not eating, less drinking
- Noticeably sleeping more
- Congestion in nose and/or throat
- Pale or grayed complexion

## DAYS OR HOURS

- Intensification of above signs and symptoms
- Sudden surge of energy and wanting to get out of bed
- Irregular or rattled breathing
- Decreased urine output
- Change in color of urine (darker)

## MINUTES

- Very irregular breathing, may stop then start again
- Cannot be awakened

## Ophelia's Story

A few days before she passed away, my mother, Ophelia, was particularly agitated and disoriented. She didn't understand why she was in the dining room and why *we* were giving her medication instead of a health care person. My younger brother looked at me a bit panicked while he began preparing her intravenous dose of anxiety reducing medication. As he walked around to one side of her, I sat down on the other. I put her hand in mine, looked her in the eyes, and began gently talking to her.

"Mom, you are safe."

"I am?"

"Yes. You are safe," I reassured her.

"Okay," she exhaled, beginning to relax.

"Close your eyes, Mom. It's okay now."

Knowing how she loved our family fishing trips, I began to slowly recreate and tell the story of one of our experiences: "It's a beautiful day outside...and we are out fishing at the lake. The sun is shining and the sky is a deep blue. It's perfect! The whole family is here...the boys are playing and laughing...Dad is casting his line and sitting in the shade of a large tree. We are all together and we are happy, enjoying the beautiful day."

I looked up at my brother and we both breathed a sigh of relief. She had fallen peacefully asleep with the sound and images of her fishing story...her three children at her side. She continued her peaceful sleep through the end of her precious life.

## dying well

*"The things you do for yourself are gone when you are gone, but the things you do for others remain as your legacy."*

KALU KALU

DYING WELL IS ABOUT personal connection and interaction. As your loved one's interest in the physical world diminishes, their life takes on a much more inward, personally significant meaning. Relationships and spirituality may be at the core of their life completion. It is essential to honour the meaningful and personal aspects of their life story.

Give your loved one the opportunity to speak with or see whomever they need to. Talk with them about your feelings. It is vital to affirm our love for one another and also to forgive each other at this most precious time in our lives.

Giving your loved one permission to go is imperative to their sense of completeness. Most importantly, let them know they are not alone and that you are going to go through this together…whatever that may look like.

# THE FINAL NESTING PLACE

## Danny's Story

After a year spent living and battling disease, Danny's young but frail body wore out. He lived his last days at home in the comfort of his own bed. The same bed he and I sat on together watching home improvement and house flipping television shows. The bed we hung out on chatting about life and who the best role models were for his nieces and nephew. The same bed where we talked openly about his dying and the heart-breaking effect it would have on his dad and others he loved. The bed where we sat and shared moments of laughter and tears now held his dying body. Danny's wife, dad, and I kept vigil by his side. We were with him when his breathing became noticeably irregular and slow. We gathered close and reassured him it was okay to leave. As he drew his final breath, he was surrounded by loved ones. Our beloved Danny died well.

## completion of life

"In the end, it's not going to matter how many breaths you took, but how many moments took your breath away."

SHING XIONG

JUST AS WE LIVE unique lives, we also die in our own unique way. It is a distinctive experience for each one of us.

If your loved one completes their life at home, consider how you will use the space in the future. Take whatever time you need to make that decision. You may choose to leave it as is. However, I encourage you to think about creating, or allowing it to evolve into, a functional living space for others to enjoy. The story of your loved one can continue to unfold and be told within the walls of their final nesting place.

## PRACTICAL MATTERS

Just as there are practical matters to attend to during illness and death, there are also things we must consider when life is complete. The immediate actions to take are:

- Allow for personal time necessary to say a final goodbye to your loved one.
- Notify the funeral home, hospice, and/or hospital/nursing home staff.
- Consider and share any plans for organ donation immediately.
- Realize and accept that your loved one's body will be removed and taken to a funeral home or morgue.
- Designate someone to notify family, friends, spiritual leaders, faith family, and colleagues of your loved one.
- Ask for any personal help you need.
- Seek assistance from funeral home staff in planning any memorial service.
- Take care of *you*.

CARRIE CHAVEZ HANSEN

## part five

## STORY OF YOU

*"What seems like the right thing to do could also be the hardest thing you have ever done in your life."*

UNKNOWN

CARRIE CHAVEZ HANSEN

## chapter eleven

## YOUR STORY

*"The theme you choose may change or simply elude you, but being your own story means you can always choose the tone. It also means that you can invent the language to say who you are and what you mean.*

TONI MORRISON

SHARING THE END-OF-LIFE experience with another being is truly remarkable and profound. The experience becomes part of *your* life story and you become its keeper. Your story, just as your loved one's story, has many unique aspects.

There are circumstances within the experience which you have no control of, but you can choose how you will respond to them. Give thought to the influence and effect these experiences have on you. Then decide...how will you choose to tell *your story*?

## care of you

*"You yourself, as much as anybody in the entire universe, deserve your love and affection."*

SIDDHĀRTHA GAUTAMA

TAKING CARE OF YOURSELF is paramount throughout your loved one's end of life and beyond. Is it selfish? Perhaps, but it is also **completely necessary** for your health and your well-being. Think of it as *self-caring*. You cannot adequately care for another person when you are not well yourself. Trust me; I know how difficult it can be to accept care of one's self during such a difficult and challenging time. But you must give yourself this grace.

- Rest when your loved one rests.
- Drink plenty of water.
- Take short breaks; go for a walk or step outside for fresh air.
- Eat healthy meals and snacks.
- Ask for help.
- Practice gratitude; name people and experiences you are thankful for.

## growing through grief

*"If ever there is tomorrow when we're not together... there is something you must always remember. You are braver than you believe, stronger than you seem, and smarter than you think. But the most important thing is, even if we're apart...I'll always be with you."*

A.A. MILNE, <u>WINNIE THE POOH</u>

LOSING SOMEONE YOU LOVE is one of the most anguish-filled experiences you will ever be confronted with. It can be debilitating and profoundly frightening. Nothing seems to makes sense or matter, and you can scarcely remember to breathe. You may feel like you'll never again be able to function in a world without them. All is not lost; there is hope in the midst of pain.

After losing both of my parents in the short span of nineteen months, I was broken. I spent many lonely days curled up in the fetal position. My life had been ripped apart and I was struggling to survive in the aftermath of their deaths. I really couldn't function anymore and I desperately needed help. I was in crisis.

A year after my mother's death, I found the courage to begin seeing a wonderful therapist named Robin. She was caring, compassionate, and understanding. Robin gave me the tools I needed to embrace and walk through my grief.

It took time and was a lot of hard work, but it was definitely worth it. We met every two weeks for a year. I am not at all ashamed of that. It was the best thing I could have done for myself and for my family. I will always be grateful to Robin for the compassion she showed me and for her commitment to help me heal.

As you begin your personal journey through grief, be kind to yourself. Give yourself the gift of time and grace. You will get through this, but it definitely takes time. It may take the assistance of a trained professional. Don't be afraid to ask for help. For me, it made an enormous difference. I have gone from merely surviving to thriving, and you can do it too.

## honouring your relationship

"*Death ends a life, not a relationship.*"

MITCH ALBOM,

<u>Tuesdays with Morrie</u>

CONTINUE YOUR RELATIONSHIP WITH your loved one by honoring it in personal and significant ways. Keeping special mementos or elements from their life story in your room gives their life a continuing story, a legacy. Photographs are a wonderful way to keep your loved one's memory close in a tangible and meaningful way.

Establishing personal rituals or creating a meaningful monument in their memory is a poignant and intimate way to honor your relationship. Whatever is meaningful and relevant to *you* and *your relationship* with them is what matters. It is your story to tell.

## CONCLUSION

"I wanted a perfect ending. Now I've learned, the hard way, that some poems don't rhyme, and some stories don't have a clear beginning, middle, and end. Life is about not knowing, having to change, taking the moment and making the best of it, without knowing what's going to happen next. Delicious Ambiguity."

GILDA RADNER

ACCEPTING THE IMPENDING LOSS of a loved one is not easy, but we can make it less hard by taking steps to create a meaningful and personally relevant space for them to live their end of life.

Embrace the path your loved one's story has taken, and be part of the culture shift that acknowledges dying as part of *living*. Transcribe their personal story by crafting a physical narrative rich in the details of their most important and profound experiences, spiritual beliefs, personal relationships, and history.

Interweave those experiences with elements of color, texture, and pattern to give them character and soul. Make something beautiful and personally tangible to enrich your loved one's end of life. Create their final nesting place™.

CARRIE CHAVEZ HANSEN

## ACKNOWLEDGEMENTS

Special thanks to Alicia Dunams for guiding and showing me that this was the story I needed to share with the world.

This book would not have been possible without the patient and loving support of my three children: Janae, Mercedes and Tristan. They didn't have to, but they chose to share me and my time with you. They are amazingly unselfish human beings. It doesn't matter how young or small they are. They have demonstrated such strength of character and love of life. I am honoured to be their mother. To my brother John Paul: for always giving me your continued encouragement and support. I appreciate your wisdom.

To my baby brother Mitch, you are the funniest person I know. Thank you for teaching me what true kindness and compassion is when caring for a loved one. To my precious boys Tono and Curt, I am proud of the men you have become and know Grandma and Grandpa would have been extremely proud as well.

To Jay, for giving me your heartfelt support; you are a wonderful father. To Judy, Dan, Sadie, Danny and the rest of the Hansen family for welcoming me into your brood and teaching me how beautiful the modern family can be. I love you all very much.

Chavez, Vialpando, Valdez, Madrid, and Valles families: Thank you for providing me with a strong sense of culture, love of God, family values, love and humor. *Te amo.*

To my amazing TRIBE of strong, smart and sexy women: Kathy Fultz, Carla Armenta Yaden, Shirley Cihura, Melissa Cusano, Amber Every, Nadine Goering and Tina Newsome. Heartfelt thanks for the many years of friendship, tears, laughter and cocktails. You ladies are my strength.

To *Juilliard, My Fairy Godmother*, and my not-so-evil *Step-sisters* at the castle: Linda Weise, Shantell Autry, Lisa Malloy, Katrina Paschal, and Margo Musante. What an incredible experience I had splashing color on the walls of the castle; I will never again look at paint the same way. P.S. I could've used some help in the dungeon.

Thanks to my Fab Fellas for amazing friendships that have stood the test of time: Tim Sheppard, I am so grateful to have you as my brother from another mother and appreciate you always wanting the best for me. Russell Munoz, thank you for believing in me, making me laugh, and for the kick ass inspiration. Randy Rotondo, your spirit of endless generosity and compassion inspires me every single day. I love you guys!

To Anita McGann for holding my hand, making me laugh, and helping to ensure my mother's wishes were honoured. Speer family: Thank you Momma Speer, Ebby, Allan Lee and Ally for loving me as one of your own.

To Rosemary and Chuck Sekera: Rose, thanks for always remembering my birthday and for the support while our mothers were battling their common disease. Chas, thanks for teaching me all the important abbreviations. P.S. The *best part* is getting to thank everyone. Leslie Jakeman, heartfelt thanks for walking with me through my darkest days.

Robin Wall, thank you for being the wind beneath my broken wings. You taught me to fly again and held me up while I was learning.

Very special thanks to my online friends and family for supporting and inspiring me on a daily basis.

CARRIE CHAVEZ HANSEN

# RESOURCES

**For additional information on preparing a final nesting place:**
THE FINAL NESTING PLACE
(719) 492-0882
carrie@thefinalnestingplace.com
TheFinalNestingPlace.com

**For information on hospice and what to expect before death:**
HOSPICE FOUNDATION OF AMERICA
(800) 854-3402
hfaoffice@hospicefoundation.org
HospiceFoundation.org

**For information about advance directives (living will and health care proxy):**
AGING WITH DIGNITY
888/5WISHES
fivewishes@agingwithdignity.org
AgingWithDignity.com

**For information on Holistic Community Living or starting an HCL home:**
HOLISTIC COMMUNITY LIVING
David Lazaroff, President
720/218-3254
david@holistic.com
HolisticCommunityLiving.org

**For information on the Music & Memory iPod Project:**
MUSIC & MEMORY
MusicandMemory.org

**For important ovarian cancer awareness information:**
OVARIAN CANCER NATIONAL ALLIANCE
*866-399-6262*
ocna@ovariancancer.org
ovariancancer.org

**For online health and wellness communities for patients and caregivers:**
INSPIRE
inspire.com

**For assistance with funerals and a national funeral home directory:**
AMERICAN FUNERAL HOMES
americanfuneralhomes.com

## ABOUT THE AUTHOR

Interior designer, Carrie Chavez Hansen, has a popular interior design internet radio show and has been featured in Denver Life Magazine. She was invited by World Market Center as one of ten top design bloggers to cover Las Vegas Market. Carrie has also been featured in a number of popular blogs and internet radio shows. She has over 15 years of residential and commercial interior design experience. When not designing or writing, she enjoys spending time with family and friends and helping her community. Carrie lives at the base of Pikes Peak in the beautiful foothills of Colorado Springs, Colorado. Carrie's philanthropic interests include raising ovarian cancer awareness through Ovarian Cancer National Alliance, Sue DiNapoli Ovarian Cancer Foundation, and Colorado Ovarian Cancer Alliance. She is also active with and firmly believes in The Colorado Springs Conservatory, and National Charity League.

www.ingramcontent.com/pod-product-compliance
Lightning Source LLC
Chambersburg PA
CBHW071127090426
42736CB00012B/2039